W9-AOY-979

BUTTERFLIES FLY

Written by Yvonne Winer

Illustrated by Karen Lloyd-Jones

ini Charlesbridge

Butterflies fly
In a dancing white cloud
That covers the fields
In a gossamer shroud.
That's how butterflies fly.

Butterflies move
Like dancers in step,
Lavish in ballgowns,
A baroque minuet.
That's how butterflies fly.

Butterflies glide
By meandering streams,
Reflecting the world
In colorful dreams.
That's how butterflies fly.

Butterflies waltz
In cloaks that gleam,
Studded with jade and
Emerald so green.
That's how butterflies fly.

Butterflies frolic
In the brisk autumn breeze,
Mingling with colors
That fall from the trees.
That's when butterflies fly.

Butterflies rest
On blossoms in spring,
While crickets chorus
And small birds sing.
That's when butterflies fly.

Butterflies take wing
In the first morning rays,
Transforming the world
With brilliant displays.
That's when butterflies fly.

Butterflies sip
Where tree frogs creep,
In gullies so gloomy,
In shadows so deep.
That's where butterflies fly.

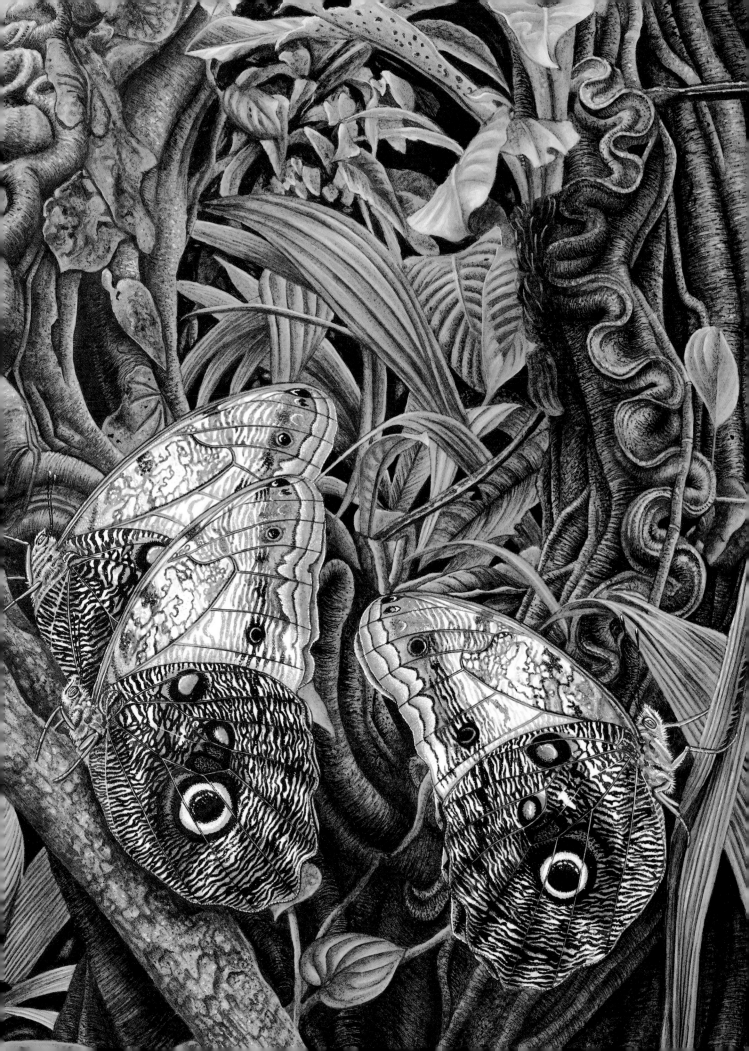

Butterflies soar
In mountains so high,
Where icy streams flow
And peaks touch the sky.
That's where butterflies fly.

Butterflies settle
On leaves beneath trees,
Camouflaged patterns
That mimic and tease.
That's where butterflies fly.

Butterflies unfold
Their swallow-tailed wings
Bedecked and bejeweled,
Like crowns fit for kings.
That's why butterflies fly.

Butterflies hover
In soft morning light:
A fragrant ritual,
An amorous flight.
That's why butterflies fly.

Butterflies dance
In crimson gowns,
Weaving splashes of color
To rainforest sounds.
That's why butterflies fly.

Butterflies paint
A palette so bright:
A gift to the world,
A symphonic flight.
That's why butterflies fly.

Butterfly Identification Guide

The earliest known butterfly fossils were found in Colorado, and are approximately 48 million years old. Sadly, butterfly habitats are being destroyed faster than we are learning about them. However, butterfly preservation is growing, as more people become interested in these lovely insects.

Butterflies undergo complete metamorphoses, over four stages: egg (ovum), caterpillar (larva), pupa (chrysalis), and adult insect (imago). While the greater part of the butterfly's life is spent as a caterpillar, it is the adult that catches the eye.

These beautiful creatures are abundant and widespread. They live in most of the world's habitats, from tundra to rainforest. They feed on a wide variety of things, including nectar, pollen, rotting fruit, dung, and other plant and animal products. Most species seek nectar from flowering plants, transfering pollen from plant to plant, helping the plant to reproduce. Colors and patterns on the wings help to protect and camouflage butterflies against predators. Some possess markings, like eyespots, which confuse enemies.

The butterflies in this identification guide are arranged in the same order as the pages of this book. The small drawing to the left is a reduction of the drawing above each poem.

Common Morpho
Morpho peleides
Central America
Wingspan 5–6 inches/12–15.6cm

This butterfly, the most common of the morphos, lives in tropical rainforests. It feeds on plants of the pea family. Both sexes are metallic blue on the upper wings, while the undersides are dark, with rows of eye-spots and a light edge.

Large White
Pieris brassicae
Europe, N. Africa, Mediterranean countries
Wingspan 2–2.5 inches/5.6–6.6cm

Over its range, this is one of the most common species, and occurs in many types of habitat. It is a widespread pest of cabbages and related vegetables. A regular migrant, it sometimes moves in large swarms.

Gulf Fritillary
Agraulis vanillae
The Americas
Wingspan 2.5–2.75 inches/6.5–7cm

This butterfly is commonly found in open spaces and gardens, visiting nectar-bearing flowers. Its wings are a reddish-orange color on the upper surfaces and spotted with silver on the underside. Also shown are two species of Daggerwings, *Marpesia chiron* (black and orange) and *Marpesia crethon*.

Blue Mountain Swallowtail
Papilio ulysses
Australia, New Guinea, Solomon Islands, New Caledonia, Moluccas
Wingspan 4–5.5 inches/10–14cm

This beautiful butterfly is generally seen around rainforests, flying high with blue wings flickering. The male will fly down to investigate any blue objects, such as clothing. The underside is dull and camouflages the butterfly when it is settled.

Emerald Swallowtail
Papilio palinurus
Burma, Thailand, Malay Peninsula, Borneo
Wingspan 3–4.25 inches/8–11cm

Predominantly green, this species is recognized by the shape and curve of the wings and the white or red spot on the edge. They spend most of their time high up among the trees, but occasionally come down to drink from puddles and damp patches on the forest floor.

Large Copper
Lycaena dispar
Europe, temperate Asia, east to the Pacific
Wingspan 1.5–1.75 inches/3.4–4cm

This is an endangered butterfly. Its habitat is exceptionally humid forests, marshes, and other water-logged environments. Many of these areas are disappearing when people drain them for other uses.

Baltimore Checkerspot
Euphydryas phaeton
Eastern N. America
Wingspan 2–2.5 inches/5–6.4cm

This is one of the largest checkerspots and it lives in wet meadows where the native turtlehead *Chelone glabra* grows. It is found throughout Maryland and its range extends from Canada to Georgia. Its populations are easily destroyed by swamp drainage and land development.

Monarch
Danaus plexippus
The Americas, Canary Islands, Indonesia, New Guinea, Australasia
Wingspan 3–4 inches/7.5–10cm

This large and powerful butterfly feeds on milkweed and uses the poisons from the plant in its own body for defence. Its markings signal that it is a toxic butterfly. Some American populations migrate thousands of miles.

Cocoa Mort Bleu
Caligo teucer
Central America and Caribbean
Wingspan 3.75–4.25 inches/9.5–11cm

These are called owl butterflies because of the big owl-like eye spots on the underside of their wings. They are among the largest of all butterflies and live in lowland rainforests. They avoid bright sunlight and fly at twilight to feed on fermenting fruit.

Apollo
Parnassius apollo
Europe, Central & Western Asia
Wingspan 2–3 inches/5–8cm

This alpine species is threatened and is protected under the Convention on International Trade in Endangered Species (CITES). The pattern of this butterfly is distinctive, but also very variable. It can be distinguished from similar species by the absence of red markings on the forewing.

Indian Leaf
Kallima inachus
Southern East Asia
Wingspan 3.5–5 inches/9–12cm

This butterfly frequently rests on the ground in leaf litter, where it becomes virtually invisible. This camouflage ability has given it its name. The upperside of both sexes is brightly colored with orange and purplish-blue, but the brown patterning of the underside and its unusual wing shape makes this butterfly an effective leaf mimic.

Common Swallowtail
Papilio machaon
N. America, Europe, N. Africa, temperate Asia, Japan
Wingspan 3–4 inches/7.5–10cm

The geographical distribution of this attractive butterfly is enormous. It inhabits meadowland and mountainsides as high as 13,000 feet (4250 meters). There are many sub-species with colors ranging from very dark blue to orange, but there is always a pair of tails on the hindwing.

Cairns Birdwing
Ornithoptera priamus
N. Australia, New Guinea, Solomon Islands
Wingspan 5–11 inches/12–28cm

This common name applies to one of a large number of sub-species. Males are distinctively patterned with black and green on the upperside. Females are much larger, and their wings are black with white markings. Birdwings have a strong gliding flight. They frequent rainforest canopies and breed on *Aristolochia* vines.

American Passion-flower Butterfly
Heliconius erato
Central America and Northern South America
Wingspan 2.25–3.25 inches/5.5–8.2cm

These butterflies fly close to the ground along forest edges and open ground. They roost communally at night. The caterpillar digests poisons from vines of the passion-flower family, which are passed on to the adult stage. Birds quickly learn to avoid them.

Australian Painted Lady
Vanessa kershawi
Australasia
Wingspan 1.75–2 inches/4.7–5cm

These butterflies are active throughout the year, but migrate southwest in the spring. They are frequent visitors to flowers and have a rapid flight. Males and females are of similar size and coloration, but the males have more angular wings.

Dedication

For Sydney, who cycles the world.
And for Michael and Judith at their magical "Firefly" in the rainforest.
May there always be butterflies. Y.W.
For my husband, Martin, with thanks. K.L-J.

Acknowledgements

Thanks to Jennifer Woodman, my colleague and friend at the University of Southern Queensland,
for years of editing, support and encouragement.
Thanks also to Geoff Monteith, Senior Curator, Entomology, Queensland Museum.

References and Recommended Reading

* *Amazing Butterflies and Moths* by John Still. New York, Knopf, 1991.
Birdwing Butterflies of the World by Bernard D'Abrera. Melbourne, Lansdowne, 1975.
Butterflies of Australia by Gary Lewis. Melbourne, Lamont Books, 1987.
* *Butterfly* by Stephen Savage. Stamford, Thomson, 1995.
* *The Butterfly Alphabet Book* by Brian Cassie and Jerry Pallotta. Watertown, Charlesbridge, 1995.
* *The Butterfly Book: A Kid's Guide to Attracting, Raising, and Keeping Butterflies*
by Kersten Hamilton. John Muir Publications, 1997.
* *Butterfly Story* by Anca Hariton. New York, Dutton, 1995.
* *An Extraordinary Life* by Laurence Pringle. New York, Orchard, 1997.
* *Flutter by, Butterfly* by Densey Clyne. Milwaukee, Gareth Stevens, 1998.
Flying Colours by Pat Coupar. Sydney, NSW University Press, 1992.
Illustrated Encyclopedia of Butterflies by John Feltwell. Sydney, Sandstone Books, 1998.
Illustrated Encyclopedia of the Butterfly World by Paul Smart. London, Salamander, 1975.
World of Butterflies and Moths by Umberto Parenti. London, Orbis, 1978.
An asterisk (*) indicates titles recommended for children and widely available.

Internet Resources

Butterflies of North America:

http://www.npwrc.usgs.gov/resource/distr/lepid/bflyusa/bflyusa.html
Sponsored by the USGS, this useful site helps identify butterflies and report sightings.

Electronic Resources on Lepidoptera—Butterflies and Moths:

http://www.chebucto.ns.ca/Environment/NHR/lepidoptera.html
An index to many butterfly- and moth-related websites.

Yahooligans Butterflies and Moths:

http://www.yahooligans.com/Science_and_Nature/Living_Things/Animals/Arthropods/Insects/Butterflies_and_Moths/
An excellent starting point for children.

First American Edition, 2001

Text copyright © 2000 by Yvonne Winer. Illustrations copyright © 2000 by Karen Lloyd-Jones.

First published by Margaret Hamilton Books in 2000.
This edition published under license from Margaret Hamilton Books, a division of Scholastic Australia Pty. Limited.
Published by Charlesbridge Publishing, 85 Main Street, Watertown, MA 02472
(617) 926-0329 / www.charlesbridge.com

Library of Congress Cataloging-in-Publication Data is available.

ISBN 1-57091-446-X (reinforced for library use). ISBN 1-57091-447-8 (softcover)

Printed in Singapore
(hc) 10 9 8 7 6 5 4 3 2 1
(sc) 10 9 8 7 6 5 4 3 2 1
The illustrations in this book were done in watercolor, gouache, and airbrush.
Typeset in 18pt Bernhard.